# 25 Negotiating Strategies of Highly Successful Women

Natalie Disque

# DEDICATION

I would like to dedicate this book to all women. May this book empower you to go after what you rightfully deserve!

# CONTENTS

Subscribe to my list! Find out about my latest books and get **discount codes** for books related to Women in Business:

http://forms.aweber.com/form/77/944045377.htm

# 1 INTRODUCTION

Negotiating in a business setting can be stressful and challenging no matter who you are, but women in the workplace face unique challenges (and possess unique skills). With this book, you'll get a complete primer on how to effectively negotiate in a variety of important situations.

Improving your negotiation skills is an essential part of making sure you can achieve everything you have worked so hard for in your career. Many women face similar problems when it comes to negotiating. However, women also have similar advantages that men are less likely to have.

Of course, it's important to remember that these gender differences are not set in stone. They are learned habits and behaviors that women have been taught from the moment we were born. That means the common mistakes from chapter 1 as well as the biggest advantages from chapter 2 likely do not apply universally to every single woman. Use your best judgement and reflect on your own personal experience to decide which do apply to you and which are not as relevant to your own situation.

  With that in mind, you can still apply the strategies in

both of those chapters as they are still good practice for anyone who is faced with a situation in which they need to use negotiation skills.

In this book, you will get a total of 25 practical strategies that you can use to become a better negotiator. By using them, you will be able to get what you deserve and be more persuasive in general.

The following five chapters are broken down into the following topics:

- The 5 most common mistakes women make when negotiating

- The 5 biggest advantages women have (but rarely use)

- 5 strategies for asking for a raise or promotion

- 5 strategies for negotiating with investors, presenting business proposals, or improving your sales

- 5 strategies to help you nail a job interview

With these 5 comprehensive chapters, you'll be better prepared to handle any situation that requires negotiation skills. So keep reading and get ready to become an even more successful businesswoman!

## 2 THE BIGGEST MISTAKES WOMEN MAKE DURING NEGOTIATIONS

The first step to becoming an expert negotiator is making sure you don't make these classic mistakes. You may not be making all 5 of the mistakes discussed in this chapter, but even one of these can hold you back enough to stop you from achieving what you really want in your career. Start taking control of your career and your future by nipping these problems in the bud.

In order to be constructive, this chapter is designed to do more than just focus on the negatives. Instead of just reading about the most common mistakes women make in a negotiation, you'll also get 5 real, usable strategies to stop making those mistakes and become a stronger negotiator.

### The Fear of Being Too Pushy or Demanding

Women tend to be much more concerned about coming off as too pushy or demanding than men are. From birth, men are conditioned by society to be more aggressive and cultivate that go-getter attitude. Women, on the other hand, are usually conditioned to be more cooperative and considerate of others.

The good news is being considerate and having that go-getter attitude don't have to be mutually exclusive! If you know you deserve something, it's not pushy or demanding to ask for it. This is especially true of the business world, where the winner is usually the one who wasn't afraid to ask for what they deserve.

This is a tough fear to get over but it's well worth the effort. There is absolutely nothing wrong with going after what you want. Instead of being afraid of seeming too pushy, be afraid of missing out on that amazing opportunity!

## Strategy #1: Know What is Fair and Expected

To help you get over this fear and get rid of that feeling that you are being too pushy, do some background research and find out exactly what is fair and reasonable to ask for. Whether it's a raise, promotion, new job, or business proposal, having an idea of what is reasonable to ask for will give you the confidence needed to know you are not being unreasonable.

This background research should include finding out what others in your position are earning on average or what qualifications others (both men and women) in the kind of job you want have. If you're looking for a loan to start a business, find out what similar businesses (which are successful) started out with so you know how much you need to ask for.

In addition to knowing what's fair, you also need to know what your negotiation partner expects during your talk. The fact is that in the world of business, a certain degree of aggressiveness is usually expected.

That doesn't mean you should throw all caution to the wind,

but don't be afraid to stand your ground and don't be afraid to walk away if you're not getting what you deserve. If you've done the research to make sure your proposition is fair and reasonable, you will find someone else who will give you what you're asking for.

## Actual Gender Bias in the Workplace

The unfortunate truth is that women who approach negotiations just as aggressively as men often are perceived as too pushy. This is a result of social conditioning and expectations. While men are fully expected to be aggressive and demand what they are worth, women are expected to be more passive and accommodating.

Yes, you just read about how you need to get over this fear of being seen as pushy or demanding. That is still true. You just also need to be aware that if you approach a negotiation with the same exact tactics that men use, you may end up dealing with this gender bias, which can hold you back. It's an unfair reality of business that will slowly change with time as more and more women enter the workforce and start competing with men as equals.

So, while you do need to get over the fear of being perceived as too demanding, you also need to take care to craft you negotiation strategy so as to avoid triggering this gender bias. It's a difficult and delicate balance, but it's certainly not impossible and each woman who successfully negotiates for what they deserve is helping chip away at this age old bias for the next generation!

## Strategy #2: Use Gender to Your Advantage

Part of this gender bias includes certain expectations about how women should behave. True or not, if you craft your strategy so as to fulfill some of those expectations, your negotiation partner will be less resistant to your request.

You've got many strategies and approaches open to you as a woman. You'll learn about five of your biggest advantages in chapter 2, so consider those as you craft your strategy for avoiding gender bias.

On the other hand, some employers want to see that aggressive go-getter attitude in their employees regardless of gender. They want to see that you can handle yourself just as well as any man in the many tough, high-stress situations that the business world is so full of.

If this is the case for your employer, craft your negotiation strategy accordingly. Show that you can, indeed, be an aggressive negotiator. As you'll learn later, negotiating is largely about playing to your negotiation partner. Know what they want and what they expect and show that you are exactly the person to do it.

## Undervaluing Self and Lack of Confidence

There have been a few studies which show that women who are negotiating on behalf of someone else will be just as aggressive as men in demanding that the other person gets what they deserve. This proves that women can, indeed, hold their own in an aggressive business world.

So why don't we see it more often? The simple answer is because women are typically too hard on themselves. In these same studies, the same women that aggressively negotiated on behalf of someone else immediately became more passive and complacent when told to negotiate for themselves.

In an effort to be modest, we tend to undervalue ourselves. If we've made a huge accomplishment, we'll assign credit to anyone or anything else before we accept that it was our own talent and hard work that made that accomplishment happen.

If that sounds like you, it's time to stop! You've got to be confident and know your own value. It's great to give credit where credit is due, but don't forget to give some of that credit to yourself! You deserve to feel proud of your achievements and to project that pride and confidence so that others know your worth.

## Strategy #3: Practice in Advance to Boost Confidence

Building up confidence and accurately valuing your own talents and abilities is definitely easier said than done. It becomes even more difficult to project a confident attitude in a negotiation situation in which you feel nervous and stressed on the inside. So how can you realistically build up confidence? Practice!

Practicing your negotiation tactics in advance will make you feel prepared and ready for the real thing. Feeling totally prepared will go a long way toward making you feel—or at least seem—more confident during the actual negotiation.

How you practice will depend on exactly what the negotiation is about but you'll get specific strategies for a variety of situations later on in this book so you can practice those to get yourself prepared.

## The Fear of Saying No

As mentioned earlier, women are conditioned to be more cooperative and accommodating than men. This means we build up an aversion to telling people "no". Saying "no" becomes even more difficult in a negotiation. What if that "no" ends the whole discussion and you walk away with nothing?

It is a risk, to be sure, but that doesn't mean you should be willing to walk away with less than you deserve. One of the tactics your negotiation partner is almost certainly going to use is offering up much less than you should be getting. Saying "no" doesn't mean you are too stubborn or uncooperative. It means you know what you want and what you have earned.

Rejecting an offer does not have to mean an end to the conversation. It just means the negotiation is not over yet. This is especially true of the first offer, which is almost always a low-ball offer used as a starting point for negotiation, rather than the final point they are willing to go to.

Do be willing to compromise and have some wiggle room on your own part, but don't let your compromising attitude lead you to accepting less than you should be getting and rightfully deserve.

### Strategy #4: The Art of the Polite No

Saying "no" is important but it doesn't have to be done in a rude or stubborn way. There are ways to say "no" without seeming pushy or uncooperative. If you're worried that rejecting an offer will leave you walking away with nothing, learn the art of the polite "no" in order to get what you deserve, while still showing that you are willing to compromise a little.

Here are a few tricks to transforming a hard "no" into an invitation for further negotiation:

- Ask for more information: say "no" to the offer and then ask for more information about their expectations and requirements.

- Provide a counter-offer: instead of just saying "no", provide a counter-offer so that your negotiation partner can get a better idea of how you can find a happy middle ground.

- Provide an explanation: if you're saying "no", you have your reasons. Explain them. Show that you are honest and fair. More importantly, show exactly why you deserve more than what your negotiation partner is offering. In many cases, they may not be aware of certain qualifications or details regarding your achievements.

- Be appreciative: say "no" with grace and appreciation. You can something like "I appreciate your making the offer but it doesn't meet my needs." Rather than just giving a blatant rejection, you are showing your consideration for the other person and your willingness to negotiate toward a deal that makes both of you happy.

- Stay in touch: if in the end, you do have to just say "no" and walk away, make sure that you show your interest in staying in touch. This simple gesture helps you avoid burning bridges and shows your negotiation partner that you have the strength to walk away from an offer that is too low, as well as the grace to accept a better offer in the future after they have had time to think. It will leave an impression and keep you in their mind for future opportunities that do meet your needs.

## Not Taking Opportunities to Negotiate

In the business world, negotiation opportunities are rarely going to come clearly labelled and asking you to go after them. You have to find or make your own opportunities. Women are far less likely to do this than men.

For example, after a major achievement, men will usually use that as an opportunity to ask for a raise or promotion. Women, on the other hand, pass up the opportunity and continue working at the same level for the same pay.

Each negotiation opportunity you pass up slows your progress. If you want to achieve your career goals, you have to actively go after it rather than just wait for others to recognize that you have earned it.

## Strategy #5: Look for Opportunities

You need to be proactive. Look for every opportunity to advance your career and make an effort to always be prepared for an unexpected opportunity to negotiate your way higher up the ladder.

After heading a major project that went off successfully or taking on more responsibilities than your current job description entails, immediately start preparing for a negotiation and then use that as your opportunity to move further up.

Initiating the negotiation while your achievements are still fresh in everyone's memory will also give you a greater advantage than if you were to wait. If you have to remind them of what you have accomplished, they are less likely to appreciate the full value you add.

Now that you've read through the most common mistakes and gotten some ideas about how you can stop yourself from making them, let's shift to a more positive note and look at the greatest advantages you have as a woman in a negotiation. In the next chapter, you'll learn about the 5 advantages you have as a woman and how you can take advantage of them.

# 3 THE BIGGEST ADVANTAGES WOMEN HAVE IN NEGOTIATIONS

The workplace is no longer a man's world. While there are still a lot of things that tend to favor men and their way of doing business, women have made a lot of progress over the past few decades. With that progress, we have put our own twist on the way business is done.

It's important to note again that, just as you may not personally be making all of the mistakes you read about in chapter two, you might not possess all of these advantages yourself. However, as a woman, you probably have at least a couple. So, why not use them?

## Cultivating Strong Relationships

Women are generally better skilled at cultivating strong relationships with people. Where men try to succeed in the business world by standing apart and showing how independent they can be, women prefer to achieve success through teamwork and embedding themselves in the social environment of the workplace.

This can be a huge advantage during a negotiation because

you can make it more than just business. As a general rule, people are more willing to agree with someone they feel a stronger connection with. That doesn't mean you need to be best friends. It just means you have a better chance of getting what you ask for if you are asking a person who feels a stronger bond with you.

It will also give you an advantage in networking which is another essential aspect of business. As much as people like to claim that business is just about profit and finding the most efficient way to run a company, it's actually founded on relationships. Companies run more efficiently when their employees cooperate as a team.

So, if you find that you are a natural when it comes to cultivating relationships and creating an atmosphere of teamwork and community, you can apply those same skills to a negotiation. You can also highlight those skills as part of the value that you add to the company during the negotiation.

## Strategy #6: Connect on a Personal Level

If you're already a natural at this, you'll have no trouble applying it to your negotiations. Look for little ways to connect with your negotiation partner(s) on a more personal level. Tell (appropriate) jokes, show consideration for their needs, find common ground.

You don't want to pry into their private life or make overt attempts to avoid business and just talk about personal matters. This will backfire on you. Instead, find ways to weave in a more personal or informal dialogue into your business negotiations. You want them to feel comfortable with you and have a pleasant experience throughout the negotiation.

This is extremely different from the traditional (male) method of aggressive cutthroat negotiating tactics. Rather than trying to overpower your negotiation partner, you are gently persuading them to align with you on a personal level so that they will also align with you at the professional level.

Lay the groundwork at the very beginning before the serious negotiating starts so that you have material to draw from later on. To do that, you can try having a small, casual conversation at the beginning. If you are in their office, look for cues like photographs, artwork, books, and other personalized details and find something you can relate with or ask about.

Throughout the negotiation, you can work on making a slightly more informal and casual atmosphere. Again, don't go overboard here. You still want to show that you take the business at hand seriously. You just want to show that, behind your professional exterior, you are a relatable and friendly person who your negotiation partner can get along with and feel comfortable around.

## Playing Your Opponent, Not Your Cards

Just as women are often better at cultivating relationships than men are, they are also better at understanding and empathizing with others. In general, we have a keener awareness of subtle physical cues that can tell us about a person's emotional state.

This can be an extremely powerful tool if you take advantage it. By knowing what sort of emotional state a person is (without needing to ask), you can better adapt your negotiation approach to work with that.

For example, if they seem to be stressed or upset, you'll know that aggressive tactics will not work as well because it will only exacerbate the negative emotions.

Whereas men might just plow ahead regardless of what state their negotiation partner is in, you have the ability to adapt and work with that emotional state. You can adopt the right tone and modify your body language in order to better suit the mood.

Doing this can go a long way toward making your negotiation partner feel more comfortable around you and put them in a generally more agreeable mood.

## Strategy #7: Read and Respond to Body Language Cues

Even if you are a natural at this in social situations, it can take some training to do it at a more conscious level. Here are some basic guidelines to reading body language during a negotiation:

- Pay attention: observe their body movements and positions carefully. How is their posture? Where are their hands? What facial expressions are they making? How does that change while listening to you? How does that change while they are speaking? If possible, make a mental note of how their posture changed when you approached. What position where they in before and how did it change when you entered? How is it changing throughout the negotiation? You want to pay attention to these details every step of the way because change in body language can tell you a lot about how they are responding to the negotiation.

- Identify constants: while observing their body language, look for consistent gestures or positions. Do they tend to rest their chin on their hand when listening to you speak? Take note. Each individual is different so you want to pay attention to what body language signals that individual is sending out. Try to take note of how their body language changes when they are resistant to what you are saying. Maybe they lean back in their chair or move their hand up to cover their mouth. You can also look for their positive response signals. They might lean forward or raise their chin slightly. There are no set in stone guidelines for what every gesture and position means but if you pay attention, you'll learn your negotiation partner's body language.

- Consider the context: remember that you are in a negotiation. In such a situation, people are naturally put up their guard a little more because they expect a sort of battle in which one person tries to take something and the other one tries to give up as little as possible. In reality, most negotiations aren't a matter of winning and losing but of cooperating. However, if you don't know each other well already, people will likely have their guard up to avoid getting taken advantage of. Don't worry if you notice this at the beginning. You can work to create a more cooperative and low-stress atmosphere by using strategies 6 and 9 from this chapter.

- Respond: once you have established what their body language is telling you, you can adapt your own body language. If they seem to be a bit defensive, modify your body language to be more open. Avoid crossing your arms, sit up straight, and keep your chin level. If they seem to be resistant to something you are saying, avoid leaning forward as this can feel a bit like an invasion on the subconscious level. In addition to adapting your own body language, you can also adapt your tone of voice and what you are saying. Find less aggressive ways of saying what you are saying if they seem resistant. On the other hand, if they seem to be responding well, continue on down that line of topic.

This strategy does take some practice, so try it out on others before you rely on it in an actual negotiation. You can start paying attention to everyone's body language and practice adapting and responding to it.

## The Listener Holds the Power

Most people think that the most important thing to do is take control of the conversation and lead it in the direction you want it to go. In reality, the more you try to take control of the conversation, the more likely you negotiation partner is going to feel threatened. Plus, you are missing out on a huge opportunity.

Rather than talking, you should be listening most of the time. Women tend to be very good listeners. In this case, listening means not only patiently sitting quietly but actively paying attention to what the speaker is saying.

It is a well-known cliché that men might be able to sit quietly, but they aren't very good at actively paying attention. Women, on the other hand, tend to be experts at this second (and most important) part of listening.

When you focus on listening, you have the opportunity to gain a lot of valuable information and better craft your strategy to suit the situation. You are also letting your negotiation partner feel that they are in control. The more they talk, the more they give away. You can use every bit of information you gain from listening in order to strengthen your own position.

## Strategy #8: Listen First, Talk Later

You don't want to be completely silent and just wait for the other person to start off on a monologue. Listening is a more active process, especially during a negotiation. Therefore, spend as much time as you can at the beginning just listening to the other person and getting a better understanding of where the both of you stand.

Ask questions and use your body language to show that you are actively listening. When it's clear that they are prompting you to give your input, keep it brief and to the point and try to bring it back around to prompt them to continue speaking.

As you are listening, gather information and strive to understand the situation as fully as possible. What mood are they in? What priorities do they have? What are their concerns? You can then use this information to craft what you say so that it directly addresses exactly the points that they need to hear. You'll have created the perfect "pitch" to sell them on your idea because you took the time to listen and get to know your negotiation partner at the beginning.

## Striving for Common Ground

Just as women generally work on building relationships, they also usually have a stronger desire to find common ground and compromises that make everyone happy. Men often approach business matters with a win-lose attitude in which they want to be the winners at all costs. This creates a more aggressive and hostile situation, which can end up making the negotiation partner feel threatened and defensive.

Using a less aggressive approach and striving for common ground can help to lower the other person's guard and put them in a more cooperative mood. This is ideal in a negotiation situation as you are more likely to get what you want, without having to aggressively force it out of them.

People are more willing to agree with someone who seems to be willing to compromise and agree with them. Nobody wants to feel like they lost, so it's better to create an atmosphere where both people come out feeling like they succeeded.

### Strategy #9: Seek Agreement, Not Victory

Right from the beginning, start looking for common ground, or at least show your interest in doing so. Look for things that you both agree on or find out what priorities and goals you share. Once your negotiation partner feels like you both share common goals and concerns, it will be easier to convince them that what you are proposing is the way to achieve your common goals.

If you are struggling to find common ground in the beginning, remember to use strategy 8 above. The more you listen, the more likely you are to pick up on something that you can use to establish common ground.

### Better Planning and Organization

As a rule, men are on the more spontaneous side while women plan and wait for the right opportunity. On the one hand, this can be a disadvantage if you allow prime opportunities to negotiate pass you by (as you read in the previous chapter).

On the other hand, this can be a huge advantage if wielded properly. Planning and organization help to make sure things run smoothly and play out how you want them to play out. Plus, the better organized you are, the more confident you will feel during the negotiation.

With the right planning and organization ahead of time, you'll be ready to handle a range of different possible scenarios and have the information you need to present yourself as a knowledgeable and capable person.

## Strategy #10: Come to the Meeting 100% Prepared

First of all, set up a meeting. If you see an opportunity to negotiate, but you don't feel ready to just jump in and get started, talk to the person to set up a meeting. This way, you are seizing the opportunity while also giving yourself the time you need to prepare and make the most out of it. People also generally like to have something scheduled in order to prepare instead of you just stopping by their office to discuss something important that is on your mind and they didn't have time to reflect on and prepare an answer for.

Once you have a meeting lined up, start getting prepared. Do all the background research you need and gather that information into one place. Create a reference sheet of sorts that you can use to keep track of the key information. You can take this to the meeting with you.

Practice your negotiation tactics on friends and family so that you are completely comfortable using them by the time the real thing is happening. Brainstorm different possible scenarios or obstacles you might encounter. What will you do if they are in a good mood? What will you do if they are in a bad mood? What will you do if they are distracted with something else? What concerns might they raise and how will you respond to them?

Of course, you can't plan out every little detail and you will have to be ready for some unexpected moments and improvisation. However, the more you plan it out in advance and the more you consider the variety of different possibilities, the more confident you will feel and the more confident you will appear to your negotiation partner.

Now that you've read through the unique sets of advantages and disadvantages you might have as a businesswoman, let's turn to focusing on applying your unique skills to real world situations. In the next three chapters, you'll learn even more strategies that are specifically geared toward specific situations you often face in the world of business.

# 4 ASKING FOR A RAISE OR PROMOTION

One of the most stressful and intimidating things you can do is ask your boss for a raise or promotion. As stressful as it is, it's something you have to get used to because most employers aren't going to take the initiative to just hand out the raise you deserve on their own.

That's not necessarily because they don't value your work. It's usually because business favors those who are proactive and go after what they want rather than waiting for it to be given to them. You aren't being demanding. You are showing your employer that you know exactly what value you add to the company. More importantly, you're also showing that you intend to continue adding more value to that company.

Here are five strategies that will help you nail this negotiation and bring you that much closer to getting the raise or promotion that you deserve.

## Strategy #11: Know Your Worth in Advance

Before asking for a raise, it's important to know how much you can and should ask for. Unfortunately, there's no magic formula that will give you the precise amount you should be earning for your work. Instead, you'll need to calculate an estimated range.

Base your figure on the amount that others at a comparable level in your company are earning. You should also do some market research to see how much people in your same job at other companies generally earn.

If you are asking for a promotion, do the same research but for the position you are hoping to get, not the one you currently have. A great source is to go to Salary.com and enter in your title and location. It will provide you with a low end, average, and high end salary for those in the same area with the same title. This will give you something to compare your salary requests to and it's an unbiased source you can mention to your boss.

Beyond your financial worth, you'll also want to create a list of your qualifications. In the case of a promotion, find out what sort of qualifications people in that position generally have. Compare those with your own qualifications. You can use this information to help convince your employer that you do, indeed, deserve that promotion.

You also want to have a list of your qualifications ready even if you are just asking for a raise. How many years have you been doing this job? How much do people generally earn when they have been working as long as you have?

When you walk into this negotiation, make sure that you don't start with the key figure you actually want. Shoot high and allow your employer to talk you down to a lower figure that is closer to the actual amount you hope to get.

By doing this research ahead of time, you will already know what range you should be in and you'll have a list of reasons you deserve it ready in case your employer doesn't see eye to eye with you at the beginning.

In many cases, your employer will probably already know about how much you should be earning and what qualifications you have. It's up to you to show that you know, too, and it's time you start earning what you have been working so hard to achieve.

## Strategy #12: Prove Your Worth

A list of qualifications will help you prove that you are actually worth what you know you are worth. However, it's also good to have a few examples. You don't want to just say "well, I've been working here for about 5 years now so I should be earning this much."

Instead, you should be pointing out concrete examples of times when you did an excellent job or went above and beyond for the company. Show them the accomplishments you have made and provide evidence of the value you have added to the company.

In some cases, your employer will already know exactly what value you have added. In others, it might not be as clear what role you played so you need to show them. If you haven't already done so, start documenting examples down. This way you are prepared.

Point out what makes you exceptional. At the same time, point out what makes you such a good fit in this specific company. You don't have to stick with hard numbers like revenue increases or sales figures. You can also talk about more qualitative value like your creativity or problem solving skills.

The important thing is to come prepared with concrete

examples of how all of your qualities and skills have benefited the company in the past.

If you are asking for a promotion, make sure to point out exactly how your skills and talent will suit the new responsibilities you want to take on. This will not only show that you are qualified but also that you know exactly what the new job position entails.

Whether it's just a raise or a promotion as well, you want to make sure you don't just focus on your past success. Past accomplishments are definitely important to bring up, but you want to be future-oriented. You want to show how this raise or promotion will benefit the company in the future.

Talk about plans you have, projects that are in the works, or training that you are currently undergoing. Talk about the goals you have for the company and the future. Keep a balance between providing past proof of your value and qualifications as well as showing your future potential.

## Strategy #13: Be Ready to Bargain

As mentioned earlier, you don't want to start at your goal figure. You want to go higher so that you can come down to the amount you actually want. This is classic negotiation strategy. Your employer will definitely be doing the same thing (except that they will start low instead of high, of course).

They are expecting you do the same thing, so don't be afraid if your high amount sounds a little too high. It should sound too high. This way, the amount you actually want will sound more reasonable.

Another good strategy, when you get down to the actual task of bargaining for the exact figure, is to wait for your employer to make the first offer. This will give you the upper hand. By letting them set the initial price point, you can estimate about how much higher they are willing to go.

It's also important to show that you are flexible. Don't stubbornly stick to a high price until they come up to the figure you want. At the same time, do not immediately except the low offer out of fear that you won't get anything if you reject it.

You can show that you know what you are worth here by asking for concessions. That is, if they seem unwilling to go up to the number you really want (but you still don't want to walk out of there with absolutely nothing), only accept the lower figure if you get other benefits in addition.

If the figure is too low, or you just get a hard "no", don't keep bargaining. Accept with grace and ask when it might be a good time to revisit the matter. A "no" now doesn't necessarily mean "no" in the future and even though you may not have succeeded this time, you'll have laid the foundations for a more promising negotiation in the future.

## Strategy #14: Use "We" instead of "I"

You want this raise or promotion to feel like something that is best for everyone involved. In reality, it actually should be something that benefits not just you but the company as well. That is, they will give you what you deserve and, in return, you will continue to strive for greater and greater success for the company.

You want to show that, for you, your success is the same as the company's success. You want to grow with the company and, at the same time, help the company to grow. This will be a lot more effective than simply saying you want the raise or promotion because you deserve it.

As true as it may be, it's not enough of an argument to convince your employer. They probably already know it's true anyway. What they want to know at this stage is how giving you a raise or promotion will benefit the company.

The best way to accomplish this feeling of mutual benefit is to watch your language. Focus on the "we" of the whole company rather than the "I" of your own self-interest. You want to embed yourself in the company and present yourself as an irreplaceable part of its future success.

By using collective language like "we" and "us", you are helping to accomplish this. You are also showing that you are primarily concerned with the company as a whole rather than just your own individual career. You are showing that you are invested in this company just as much as your employer is.

## Strategy #15: Be a Problem Solver

Asking for a raise or promotion presents two key problems to your employer. First, they have to figure out where to get the money for that raise. Secondly, in the case of a promotion, they have to figure out how your previous responsibilities will be handled once you step up into your new position.

Once you have proven that you deserve it and shown how it can benefit the company as well, the only concerns that are likely to remain are these two. So drive your point home by being ready with solutions.

Find ways to address these concerns and show that these obstacles will not be an issue. Show how you will add enough value to more than offset the cost of the raise. Discuss the potential of training a colleague to fill in for your old position (or the option of continuing in that position yourself) until the company finds a replacement.

By showing that you have already considered these issues and come ready with potential solutions, you are putting your employer at ease while also providing evidence of your foresight and problem solving skills.

Asking for a raise or promotion should be a little less nerve-wracking now that you have the strategies you need to handle the negotiation like a pro. Read the next two chapters to get even more strategies for other tough negotiation situations you might face in your career.

# 5 BUSINESS PROPOSALS, SALES, AND INVESTOR MEETINGS

As a business owner, entrepreneur, or even a saleswoman, you're in a position where strong negotiation skills are essential. If you want someone to invest their hard earned money in your ideas, you've got to present yourself as someone they can trust and someone who can follow through on their promise.

As with everything in life, practice makes perfect. During a presentation, investor meeting, or sales call, you want more practice than ever to avoid sounding uncertain and unprepared. Use the strategies in this chapter to help give you the upper hand in any of these negotiation situations.

## Strategy #16: Show Both Objective and Subjective Worth

In business, it's easy to think that value can only be measured in objective numbers. But subjective qualities that can't be measured in numbers are just as valuable.

The relationships you build with the people you work with, the productive and positive atmosphere you help to create, and all the little extra things you do to be a better employee and help the company are just as important as the objective figures you can show about the value you bring.

This is not to say that those numbers aren't important. They certainly are. But these appeal to people's reason only. In many cases, the difference between landing the deal and getting declined are those subjective feelings people have about you.

Your subjective worth, in this case, are qualities like honesty, trustworthiness, dependability, respect, and consistency. You want to show that you are someone they can work with and rely on.

So bring them the hard data, but remember to show your subjective qualities as well. Be courteous and considerate toward your negotiation partner(s). Show up on time. In fact, be early. Turn your phone off and give them your undivided attention. Listen to their concerns and give meaningful responses.

## Strategy #17: Cultivate a Persona of Honesty and Openness

In many ways, this could be considered similar to the previous strategy. Honesty and openness are subjective qualities that you want to embody during your negotiations. However, these are so important, it's worth giving them their own special mention.

All too often, business gets a bad reputation as being full of dishonest people who will stop at nothing for more profits. You will certainly meet people like this. It's important to set yourself apart and show that you care deeply about the business, not just the profit.

Your negotiation partner needs to see that you are honest and open in order to trust you. Without trust, it doesn't matter how convincing and well-crafted your pitch is, they aren't going to believe a word of it.

Establish a persona of honesty and openness right from the very beginning. Provide real, honest data. Point out potential concerns before they have a chance to bring them up and address them. When they bring up a concern you haven't mentioned, respond to it honestly and meaningfully. Don't just try to write it off as unimportant or not worth worrying about.

They need to feel like they are getting the full story, not just the positive headlines. Let them know that they can trust you by giving real, honest answers. You don't have to undersell yourself or make yourself look bad. Just show them that you aren't ignoring potential issues and concerns. They will feel more secure about the future knowing that you are the sort of person who faces problems head on rather than just trying to pretend they don't exist.

## Strategy #18: Choose Your Targets Wisely

The fact is, you can't win everybody over and there's really no reason to try. Rather than spreading yourself thin by trying to appeal to ever single potential investor or customer, do your research and narrow down your list to focus only on your very best leads.

You are going to have more success if you focus on fewer targets who are more likely to be interested and share your values and goals. This is mainly because, with fewer targets, you have more time and energy to invest in presenting your very best self to each of them rather than coming in frantic and half-prepared to each meeting, trying to remember who it is you're talking to this time.

Learn as much as you can before you even set up a meeting. Find what their needs, interests, and expectations are. Know what potential concerns or hesitations they might have and be prepared to address them thoroughly and honestly.

During the meeting itself, continue to listen and observe so that you can learn more about the people you are talking to. Pay attention to how they are responding to what you say (both their verbal responses and their body language).

When you know you already share similar values and goals, you'll have a much easier time speaking to them in their own language and telling them what they need to know in order to say yes.

## Strategy #19: Project Confidence

Projecting confidence during this kind of negotiation is just as important as presenting yourself as honest and open. If you don't seem confident in what you're saying, how can you expect them to feel confident enough to say yes?

Negotiations like these can be extremely nerve-wracking. Often, you've got a lot on the line and you really, really want to get that yes. This can put you on edge as you stress about saying the right thing. You need to do your absolute best to push down those nerves and anxious thoughts and put on a brave face.

This can be especially difficult as a woman, since you have likely been conditioned to be a little more modest and reserved. This modesty can easily be mistaken for a lack of confidence, however. In business, it is often better to err on the side of being overly-confident rather than too modest.

People need to see that you believe in yourself just as much as you want them to believe in you. So do whatever you need to do to feel more confident.

Long before the meeting actually takes place, you should make sure you prepare yourself. Create a plan. Identify which strategies you are going to use. Brainstorm potential topics and issues that will be brought up. Plan out as many details as you can and then practice.

On the day of, if you've got a lucky pair of shoes or favorite shade of lipstick, wear them. Put your favorite outfit on. Put your hair up so you don't nervously play with it. Eat a good breakfast. Show up early so you have a little time to adjust to your surroundings and get comfortable.

Do everything in your power to reduce your stress levels and show up feeling calm, collected, and confident.

## Strategy #20: Don't Give Up After Being Told No

In some cases, no matter how amazingly well you did or how sure you were that they would say yes, you are still going to hear "no". Stay calm! This is not the end of the world and it's certainly not the end of your career.

During negotiations, especially if you are negotiating with men, people tend to feel an increased pressure to be tough and aggressive. They will say "no" as a default. In some cases, it really does mean "no". In other cases, it actually just means the negotiation is not over.

While you don't want to be too pushy or bother the person, it's perfectly acceptable to follow up with someone even after they have said "no".

Allow the current meeting to come to a close. Accept their

response with grace and dignity and then follow up with them by writing an email on the same day or the day after. Don't push them too hard to reconsider, just thank them for their time and say that you look forward to another opportunity to speak with them again.

Ending on a positive note will ensure that they think of you in a positive light. They may have said "no", but later on down the road, they might be in a better position to say yes and when they are, they will remember you.

Therefore, remember to always be courteous and respectful and, above all, be persistent. Just because they said "no" now does not mean that bridge is burned.

The strategies we just discussed will help you power through even the toughest of negotiations but perhaps the most nerve-wracking negotiation you'll ever go through is the very first one you have to do: the job interview! In chapter 5, we'll look at five unique strategies for helping you ace that job interview and get you started on your career path.

# 6 JOB INTERVIEWS

The job interview is the first and, in many ways, the most important negotiation you'll ever engage in. In fact, the first step to a successful interview is understanding that it is, indeed, a negotiation.

Many of us tend to think of it as a high stress situation in which we have to desperately show the potential employer that we deserve the job above every other candidate. While proving you deserve the job is part of it, the interview is not a one-way street. It's just as much a chance for you to get to know the potential employer and decide if the company is a good fit for you. Relax and think of it as more a conversation than in inquisition.

When you walk in as a negotiation partner rather than an interview candidate, you're already making a strong first impression that will set you apart from the rest. Beyond that, use these five strategies to navigate that interview like an expert.

## Strategy #21: Show and Tell What You Will Offer

In a job interview, your potential employer knows very little about who you are. Unless for some reason they have met you before, all they really know for sure is what you've said on your resume.

That means that you can't leave anything to chance. You need to use that first face to face meeting as your prime opportunity to make a fantastic first impression. Talk about your unique talents and accomplishments. Be confident and don't be afraid to sell yourself.

It may feel a little bit awkward, especially if you are used to being modest. But remember, this person knows almost nothing about you. If you don't make a point to talk about it, they never will.

In addition to talking about your accomplishments and talents, you also need to show yourself to be the person you say you are. Sit up straight, smile, and speak with confidence. Embody that amazing, open, honest, and accomplished person that you are!

## Strategy #22: Find Ways to Relate More Personally

As a woman, you probably have a natural ability to relate with people on a more personal level. This is an important talent to use during your job interview. This interview is a chance for both you and your employer to get an idea of what it would be like to work together.

If you are friendly and get along well, your potential employer will know that you have a strong chance of fitting in well with the rest of your future coworkers. While the employer certainly wants an individual who possesses unique talents and skillsets, they also want someone who will work well in a team with others. More specifically, someone who will work well with the others who already work there.

You don't want to make too many obvious attempts to get personal. If you do, the strategy could end up backfiring as the person feels like you are getting too personal or avoiding the important questions.

Instead, add a slight personal note to the beginning and the end of the interview. At the beginning, look for something in the office you can comment on or strike up a short, casual conversation about something that happened.

At the end, you can use the information you have gathered from listening throughout the interview to come up with something personalized (but, again, not overly personal) to say.

The friendlier you are, the more easygoing the interview will be and the more relaxed you will feel. This will also help to make you feel more confident and present your very best self.

## Strategy #23: Let the Employer Make the First Offer

If the interview goes well and the employer wants to offer you the job, wait for them to set the starting salary figure. You don't want to accept this offer since it is almost certainly going to be on the lower end.

They will expect a negotiation here so don't be afraid to actually negotiate for the salary you really want. Just make sure you wait for them to put the starting bid on the table. This gives you the opportunity to get a sense of around how much they expect to actually pay you and to develop an argument for why you deserve the amount you actually want.

Decline politely and provide the reasoning behind why you declined before presenting your counteroffer. Be confident and calm during this part of the negotiation. Don't be afraid to walk away from the job entirely if the employer is not willing to give you what you are truly worth.

If they are offering you the job, it means they know you would be a valuable addition to the company. It's not unreasonable to ask that you be paid an amount that reflects that value. As mentioned in earlier chapters, it's a good idea to do your research ahead of time and know about how much you should expect to get paid.

This first negotiation of your salary is your chance to establish yourself as a strong candidate. If you accept that first offer, you are likely undervaluing yourself which could make that potential employer doubt how much you are really worth.

## Strategy #24: Ask Questions

You have probably heard this before but it is absolutely essential that you come ready to ask questions during the interview. The questions you ask are what show that you are knowledgeable about the position you would be taking. It also gives you a chance to turn the tables a bit and interview the employer to find out if the company would really be a good fit for you.

A potential employer wants to see that you are just as concerned about finding the right company for you as the company is about finding the right person to bring onto the team. You are not just hunting a paycheck or trying to take the first job that comes your way, you are actually seriously considering the opportunities you have.

It's a good idea to have two questions ready before the interview so that you know for sure you have some questions you can ask. But if you find an opportunity to ask a question based on something the employer has said during the interview, take it. This will allow you to turn the one way interview into a more natural two way conversation and level the playing field a bit.

## Strategy #25: Prioritize

When negotiating a potential job, you need to have a clear idea of your expectations and priorities. You also need to rank them in order of importance. This will benefit you in many ways.

First of all, it will give you a clear idea of what you actually want in your new job. For example, is it more important to have opportunities for advancement or a high starting salary? Do you want a job that can turn into your career or are you just looking to gain some real world experience before you set off on your own?

There are many different priorities that job seekers have when they apply for a job. You probably have multiple reasons yourself. Write them down and rank them in order of priority.

Secondly, having your priorities clearly set out in your mind will allow you to handle the interview with confidence and ask pointed, clear questions. You'll also be able to give stronger, more concrete responses to the employer's questions because you will have a stronger understanding of your own goals and expectations.

Finally, it gives you the ability to compromise. For example, if your top priority is to have opportunities for career advancement, you can give yourself a little more wiggle room on the salary. Keep this in mind when you are ranking your priorities so you already know where you are willing to compromise.

With the 25 strategies you have learned in these five chapters, you are now ready to tackle even the toughest of negotiations. All that's left for you to do is choose the ones that suit your own unique skillset best and then practice, practice, practice!

# 7 CONCLUSION

If you had to sum up all the strategies in this book into one key takeaway lesson, you might say it's: Prepare, Practice, and Present. In other words, the most important thing to do in order to be an effective negotiator is to *prepare* by doing research and gathering all the information you need; *practice* the different tactics and arguments you will use; and, finally, *present* yourself as confident and deserving of everything you are asking for.

As a woman in the workplace, you also have to take care to apply your unique advantages every step of the way. As a better planner and organizer, the "prepare" stage will likely be the easiest for you. This is a huge advantage because being well-prepared will not only ensure that you are ready for whatever comes up during the negotiations but also gives you the confidence you need to be a strong negotiator.

Practicing your tactics and arguments is important for everyone but even more so for women, especially if you struggle with building up the confidence to negotiate for what you deserve. The more you practice, the less nervous you will be and the more smooth and natural you will sound during the actual negotiation.

Finally, negotiations ultimately come down to presentation. No matter how much you may deserve that investment, raise, or job, you simply won't get it if you can't effectively present yourself as a deserving candidate. This is where women tend to struggle the most. You may be a hard worker and extremely smart and talented but, as a woman, you might naturally be more modest about your qualifications and skills than a man would.

Before your next negotiation, take the time to do an honest self-assessment. What are your personal strengths and weaknesses when it comes to negotiating? Use this book to develop a set of strategies that help to both bring out your unique strengths while targeting and working on your weaknesses.

Now, get out there and use your new negotiation skills to demand you get everything you have been working toward in your career!

# ABOUT THE AUTHOR

Natalie Disque is a PMP certified full time IT Project Manager who has worked in the IT department for many clients such as Capital One, Bank of America, Wells Fargo, Prudential Relocation, and Johnson & Johnson Canada. Due to her many business contracts throughout the years, Natalie has learned the fine art of negotiating. This book includes just some of the main 25 negotiating strategies as a woman that she believes you should know and use to get what you want in life.

Natalie resides in the Chesterfield Virginia area. You can connect with Natalie on LinkedIn: https://www.linkedin.com/pub/natalie-disque-pmp/5/202/717